WAYS TO MAKE MONEY FROM HOME

EXPLORE ONLINE AND OFFLINE OPPORTUNITIES TO MAKE MONEY FROM HOME

CHARLIE NEWMAN

To my Father, Mother, and Guide

to whom I shall remain indebted

for setting the foundation on which

all my books are inspired.

Contents

CHAPTER I

Introduction

Making money from home is one of the most cherished ideas for almost all populations. For some, it is a need; for others, it is a choice.

Everyone's dream is to make money from home. In fact, this is how our ancestors used to make money a long time ago. Long ago, most people were either farmers or small-scale home-run entrepreneurs. Of course, there were some small numbers of migrant workers too, but we will ignore them in this context.

But, with the advent of the industrial age, employee culture started booming, and with that came huge employee migration and the construction of metro cities to support them. This culture is still alive today and, in fact, it is dominating the world. Nowadays, all countries' economies are mainly concentrated in their selected metro cities or states.

With concentrated economies come a slew of issues, such as migration, quality of life, stress-related issues, higher living costs, and a lower standard of living. Even the education system is now almost finetuned for creating employees rather than entrepreneurs in most cases. That does not mean the current education system is bad. It was just the necessity of that time, so that is what has continued till today.

Because of this, most people, after completing their education, migrate to cities for work and leave behind their families, land, houses, and sometimes happiness.

Good or bad, the world population is now adjusted to this system. That does not preclude you from earning a living from home.

People have started to realise the problems in concentrated economies, and they are looking for a way to make money from home.

In this book, I have brought out many different ways through which you can make money from your home. Some ways may suit you and some may not. My job is to bring it out in as many ways as possible. Your responsibility is to choose what suits you and stick to it.

So, don't rush. Please read this book carefully. Read all the chapters and decide what works for you based on your talent, interest, skill set, budget, time availability, physical condition, etc., then make decisions.

CHAPTER II

This Book is Best Suited for

Type 1: Those who aspire to or wish to work from home.

- People who are fed up with long commute times to the office.
- People who live in big cities are fed up with pollution, low-quality food, costly lifestyles, low savings, etc.
- People who miss their family and have to take a long drive or flight to visit them.
- People who like to create other sources of income apart from their regular jobs.
- Housewives.
- Retired and old people.
- Etc.

Type 2: Those who have no other choice but to work from home.

- physically handicapped people.
- People who have been in an accident and cannot travel.
- People who are unable to cover the cost of working outside the home.
- People who have kids to take care of at home, especially single moms,
- People who live in remote locations or islands
- People who have lost their job and moved back to their native places to save expenses.

- Some unplanned situations, etc.

CHAPTER III

Advantages

The best part about making money working from home is that you save commute time. Trust me, you do not know what it means unless you are from any metro city like New York, Bangalore, Dubai, or similar cities.

People literally spend hours daily in traffic just to serve others. This not only wastes their valuable time but also has an impact on their health and emotional state.

Some of the important advantages of making money working from home are:

- You can save commute time (perhaps this is the biggest saving).
- You can reduce unnecessary expenses like Teatime expenses, Travel expenses , Junk food and parties , Other comparable costs
- You can spend more quality time with your family.
- You can save on rent and other travel expenses. This is where you make a real fortune. Rent and travel expenses consume the majority of the working population's income. By saving that, you can divert it to a good investment for future returns.
- Saving will be more. Based on the above,
- You can use that extra time to learn something new. Since you will be able to save lots of time, like commuting time, getting ready for the office, etc., You can use that for your personal productivity.
- There is no one to monitor you or restrict you in any way physically.
- Home-cooked food (Trust me, it makes a huge difference in your health condition).

- The best part is that you can choose your work environment based on your preferences and budget.

etc

CHAPTER IV

Problems and Challenges

Just because you make money from home does not mean it will be the best way and the situation will always be positive. There are some problems and challenges too. Let us see what those are.

Most of the time, people in the excitement of making money from home end up being at home for a long time and cut themselves off from the outside world. This creates a lot of problems that do not pop up initially but eventually add up to become big problems.

Some Problems and Challenges with Making Money from Home

- Making money from home takes time and patience, and it is not a piece of cake for all.
- It is difficult to maintain consistency in whatever you do.
- Making money from home is possible, but not consistent. Some days are good, and some days are bad. Sometimes you may have to change the business itself (assuming you are not doing a WFH job for any company).
- Often, you will feel a disconnect from the outside world. This is because, normally, you may get too busy working in your room and then spending time with your family at home that you may end up with no time for your side stuff or friends. (This is not true for everyone, but it is true in the majority of cases.)
- Difficulty in maintaining discipline while working. Self-monitoring is one of the toughest jobs in the world. Do you not believe in me? Try to control yourself for a month on any task and see what happens.
- Productivity issues Again, this is because of a lack of discipline and related problems.

- maintaining a balance between family and work.
- health issues because of a lack of travel.
- Self-monitoring becomes the biggest problem in the long run.
- The Problem of Boredom Humans are social animals. Since you spend almost all your time at home during work, you may start to feel damn bored over time.
- It is difficult to separate work and family problems because of a lack of distance.
- You may end up losing friends.
- You will lose the opportunity to understand the outside world, people, and the market.
- Stagnation.
- family conflicts.
- Earning capacity is not so great for work-from-home jobs or businesses.

Problems and challenges are inevitable. What you have to do is find out how to overcome them if you wish to continue making money from home.

CHAPTER V

Success Formula

If you wish to succeed in making money from home, then you may have to adopt and follow the following principles.

Time & Patience:

Making money from home needs patience. If you are a salaried employee, then that is a different case. But, if you are planning to make money through some business, then it needs time and patience.

It takes time to establish your business. Big or small , it does not matter. People do not trust any business unless they are convinced of that. So, be willing to spend time with that business and be willing to wait patiently till it generates money.

Remember, whatever it is, it will take time.

Discipline:

Normally, if you are a salaried employee or, in any other case, managed by a manager, you will be disciplined as compared to other people.

This is exactly the opposite when you work from home and no one is monitoring you.

Making money is different from making money consistently. To make money consistently, you need discipline.

Humans are lazy by default. We always try to find reasons to relax. This is especially dangerous when you are at home alone. Productivity in work-from-home environments is very low for many people. So, please maintain strict discipline and follow it if you wish to make money.

Discipline needs habit change. You can read more on this topic.

A Clear Goal:

If you are planning to make money on your own without joining any company, then I suggest you have a clear written goal.

There are hundreds of ways through which you can make money from home. But, you do not have time to try all of those.

To write a clear goal, you must first understand and be clear about what you want and do not want. Understand what your needs, interests, and passions are and then select the business or job that suits your passion.

Then, make a goal plan. Decide what business you want to do and what products and services you want to produce and serve. Also, plan on how you make money from that business and how much.

Without this, please do not start whatever you want to start. Because we all know that failing to plan is nothing but planning to fail.

Consistency & Commitment:

Starting something and making it successful demands discipline, good planning, consistency, and commitment.

The biggest problem with people is that they are not consistent. Today they work well, and they ignore it tomorrow, and they forget the day after tomorrow. If you want to make money from home, then this is not the way you want to work.

Though making money from home may not be as professional as big corporate companies, you may have to still run it like a business. And the success of any business demands consistency and commitment.

To be consistent in any business, you must first love that business. You have to be passionate about it. If you are not passionate about it, then eventually you get bored and when things go off-road you will quit instead of trying hard to resolve it.

If you are not willing to spend time with that business when it is in bad shape, then you better sign off on the business and move on to something better.

Confidence.

A big problem with making money from home is that you may or may not get help when needed. Most of the time, people do not trust us or believe in our process of making money from home.

Let us not blame them because that is how they are programmed. It is called an employee mindset. That is why you have to have confidence in yourself no matter what.

Trust in your business and your process. It is okay if you fail in the beginning. But eventually, you will succeed if you believe in yourself.

Hard work with smart guidance.

Money does not grow on trees. You have to earn it. For that, you have to work hard. It does not matter where you put that hard work: at home or outside.

Hard work is a must, but if you can add smart guidance to it, then you can reduce your time to success and increase your earning potential.

Some examples of smart guidance are:

- Take proper coaching before starting any business.
- Keep in touch with the people who are already successful in your business and in this process.
- Keep updating your knowledge.
- Re-invest in your business.
- Etc.

CHAPTER VI

Ways to Make Money from Home

There are hundreds of ways through which you can make money from home. All you have to have is creativity and an open mindset. That's it.

In this book, I have brought out some of the ways through which you can make money from home. This list is very important and has a high potential for earning enough money to live on. Also, there are some ways that, when done properly, can make you a millionaire.

Please note that this list is not final and you can come up with many more ways to make money from home. Whatever I have mentioned here is based on my studies and personal experience.

In short, I have divided this subject into 3 parts.

- Making Money from Home Through Online Means (Suited for those well-versed and skilled in computer-related stuff)
- Making Money from Home Through Offline Means (for those who lack the knowledge and skills of the computer, internet, and related technology)
- Making money from hybrid means, i.e., through both online and offline activities,

You can also adopt a hybrid approach to start offline and then move online. Let us discuss each one of the meanings in detail.

CHAPTER VII

Online Ways to Make Money

Making money online is one of the booming trends. In fact, most of the new rich millionaires that you find in the market (at least most of them) made their fortunes through online businesses like blogging, mobile app businesses, software services, social media, etc.

This means it has huge upside potential and very little downside risk. In fact, if you master online business, you can become a millionaire, and if you develop special applications like Facebook, Amazon, and Tik-Tok App, you can become a billionaire too (that is rare but possible).

But there is a catch here. Not everyone is capable of making money from online means. This needs internet access and computer literacy. Unfortunately, most people still do not have this skill set or they have to learn this skill from the beginning, inside out.

If you really do not understand online business, then no need to worry. There is a section dedicated to making money from home through offline means and you can check that out. However, I recommend that you read this section because you never know what ideas or motivation you will gain from it.

Anyways, let me list out the possible options to make money from home through online means. Again, I am telling you, this is not the final list but a reference list and there may be more ways in which I may have missed out.

Ways to Make Money from Home Through Online Means:

- Blogging & Website Design.

- Affiliate Marketing
- mobile app development business.
- digital products and services.
- Product flipping (blogs, products, etc.)
- YouTube
- Online teaching
- Freelancing.
- Podcasting.
- Book Publishing.
- software jobs.
- Stock market
- Sell & Videos photos online.
- E-Commerce.
- Domain Flipping
- Digital Marketing.
- A Virtual Assistant
- Etc.

Let us discuss each one in detail.

• • •

7.1 Website Development and Blogging

What is blogging?

Have you ever searched anything on Google and read any articles on any subjects you are interested in? If your answer is yes, then that is nothing but a website or a blog. Writing useful information on a website in the form of an article is called "blogging," and each one of those articles is called a "blog."

And for those who do not have any idea of online surfing, blogs are nothing more than digital versions of newspapers, magazines, etc. Writing these blogs or articles is called blogging. (Though the definition of blogging is more complex, if you understand this much, then it is fine as of now).

Requirements to Start Bogging

- First and foremost, you have to be digital literate.
- Need a topic or a niche to start a blog?
- You should have an internet connection and a laptop for blogging.
- You should have some writing skills and immense patience to write blog posts.
- Need some initial capital (around $200) to host a blog and make it live. There are platforms like Blogger.com that allow people to start blogging for free too.
- You should have some knowledge of blogging, and for that, you can read books on blogging (Check out my other books on the same subject), do some research, or join a blogging course.
- Finally, you should have patience and time to wait for your business to take shape. Remember, this business needs a minimum of 6 to 10 months of time to show real results.

Ways to Make Money from Blogging?

Once your blog ranks well in search engines and attracts sufficient visitors, you can start monetizing your blog using the below-mentioned resources.

- Use advertisement networks like Google AdSense, Infolinks, etc. to serve ads on your blogs. These advertisement networks serve ads on your blogs and, in return, they share part of their revenue from those ads.
- Make money using affiliate marketing. In affiliate marketing, you share a link to a product you would like to promote to the

visitors of your blog. When they buy that product through your link, you get a commission from that sale.

- You can sell your own digital products (like e-books, online courses, etc.) on your blog and make money.
- You can sell blog post space for private advertisements to make good money.
- You can also make money from guest blogging.
- You can make money by writing reviews for third-party products.
- You can even sell your blog and make money.
- And many more.

Initial Investment or Capital?

Blogging definitely needs some initial capital, but that is a very minimal amount. To start a blog, you usually need to spend money on a hosting server, a domain name, a WordPress theme, an SSL certificate, and so on.

Overall, you may need around $200.

Time to make your first $100?

Blogging needs a minimum (on average) of 6 to 10 months of time to give results. As per my prediction, you may have to wait around 9 months for your first $100, and after that, your income will gradually increase.

Earning Potential

Blogging has a huge earning potential. There are thousands of bloggers out there who make millions of dollars every year just through blogging. The best part about blogging is that you can start your blog and make money while sitting at home. Also, blogging has been one of the best ways to generate passive income for a long time. On average, you can make 2000 to 5000 dollars per month over time.

Can this be a source of passive income?

Of course, yes. But to reach that stage, you may have to work very hard.

Does this have the potential to make you a millionaire?

Yes. There are plenty of bloggers who are now minting money in the millions from blogging. But, do not forget that to reach that stage, they have spent enough time, hard work, and patience.

For more study refer to these Blogs:

- https://www.theblogstarter.com/
- https://www.bloggingbasics101.com/
- https://neilpatel.com/
- https://www.wpbeginner.com/
- https://www.shoutmeloud.com/
- https://moz.com/
- https://www.searchenginejournal.com/
- https://www.searchenginewatch.com/

• • •

7.2 Affiliate Marketing

What is Affiliate Marketing?

Affiliate marketing is a commission-based business model. In affiliate marketing, you share a link or coupon code for a product you would like to promote to your targeted audience through means like email, social media (like Facebook and YouTube), blogs, or through advertisements or direct link transfer.

When someone buys that product through your link or uses the coupon code you shared while buying that product, you get a commission from that sale.

This is very simple in terms of understanding but a bit complex in practical implementation.

Affiliate Marketing Requirements

- You have to be digital literate.
- You need to have knowledge about computers, the internet, and affiliate marketing products.
- Please spend some time learning affiliate marketing, then jump into business. You can go through YouTube videos for quick understanding, or you can buy books or join any online or offline course for the same.
- You need a computer and internet facility to start this business.
- You need marketing skills to persuade your target audience.

How Can I Make Money Through Affiliate Marketing?

Here are some ways through which you can make money:

- You can share your affiliate coupon code via the mouth, phone, email, blog, or social media.
- You can use affiliate links on your blogs, social media pages, etc.
- You can run ads on Facebook, Instagram, etc. to promote the affiliate product.

- You can even innovate more ways to reach people, but before that, make sure to read the affiliate regulation guidelines of the product or company you are promoting.

  Some good affiliate marketing networks:

- CJ Affiliate
- Amazon
- ClickBank
- ShareASale
- Etc

  Also, you can join individual product affiliate networks like:

- GoDaddy
- HostGator
- Bluehost
- Theme Forest
- etc

Initial Investment or Capital?

To be frank, you do not need anything other than a laptop or mobile, an internet connection, and time to invest.

Time to make your first $100?

If you are active enough in this business, you should be making your first $100 within one or two months.

Earning Potential

Many bloggers have become millionaires because of affiliate marketing.

It has the potential to make millions. But on average, you should be making 1K to 3K per month without any problems.

Can this be a source of passive income?

Of course, yes. But to reach that stage, you may have to work very hard. I can say this is a semi-passive income business as you have to keep updating new products and links to maintain income.

Does this have the potential to make you a millionaire?

Yes. But it takes lots of effort, consistency, and time.

• • •

7.3 Mobile App Development Business

What is a Mobile App Development Business?

If you have an iPhone or Android phone, then you know what mobile applications are. Each and everything that you use on these phones is nothing more than an application of one or other form.

Developing a mobile application based on interest or based on demand is nothing but a mobile development business.

Developing a mobile application is an industry in itself, and it is a multibillion-dollar industry. Personally speaking, this industry has a huge potential to make money and will also help provide employment to others.

What are the prerequisites for starting this business?

- You should have a laptop or computer.
- internet connection.
- mobile application software development knowledge.
- Spare mobile to test your application.
- time and patience.
- Creativity.

Ways to Make Money from Mobile Applications

- Display advertising in your mobile application using advertising networks like Google AdMob, etc.
- Using an affiliate product link
- Develop applications and sell them for profit.
- Sell digital products through in-app purchases.
- Develop a mobile application for others.
- Create a subscription model for your application (these days all software is moving in this direction and it is also called a "pay and use model").

Initial Investment/Capital

The only investment you may have to make is to pay the joining fees of the advertisement network (mostly 25 to 50 dollars).

Mobile development software tools as well as mobile app development tutorials are completely free.

Time to make your first $100?

5 to 9 months, depending on the application type and its category.

Earning Potential

If you're good, it can fetch you an average of 500 to 2000 dollars per month.

Can this be a source of passive income?

Yes, definitely. More applications, more money.

Does this have the potential to make you a millionaire?

Yes. The mobile application development business is an industry in itself. And with the advent of smart mobile phones, now almost all online transactions are done online through mobile phones.

So, I suggest you consider this option a bit more serious than the other.

• • •

7.4 Digital Products and Services

What are digital products and services?

Digital products are nothing but useful resources like software, applications, music, etc., which are in digital software form.

Though they do not have any physical shape, they are useful in their own way.

Examples of digital products:

- Software.
- Videos

- Movies
- Courses.
- eBooks
- audio and video music, etc.

Digital services are the same as digital products, but they differ in their usage and consumption patterns.

Normally Digital products are downloadable and you can use them locally, with or without the internet. However, digital services are typically not downloadable, are only available online, and are consumed on-demand.

Examples of digital services:

- Websites.
- Podcasts.
- Google Docs, PowerPoints, etc.
- Online Games
- Online Video Editor, Converter, etc.

Requirements?

- laptop with the internet.
- very good development knowledge of digital products and services.

If you are from a software background, then this may be your field to make some good money.

If you do not have that much knowledge, then you can form a partnership with someone who is good at digital stuff and make some products and services and share the profit. Well, in short, you can hire someone to work for you.

Are There Ways to Make Money from Digital Products and Services?

- Sell your digital products like software, photos, music, etc.
- You can even rent the digital products.
- Make money through subscription-based services.
- royalty-based income. EG: Permission to use photos, videos, fonts, etc. and taking a share in the sale.

Initial Investment/Capital

- computer or laptop with an internet connection.
- knowledge of digital products.
- Skills in Software Design and Development
- Creativity.
- time and patience.
- Use marketing skills to market your products and services (You can use digital marketing modalities to market your products and services online).

Time to make your first $100?

It depends on the type of product and services. But you should be making your first $100 within the first 4 to 6 months.

Earning Potential

This has a very huge potential to make money. If everything goes well, you will make money in the millions.

On average, you should make somewhere between 1K and 4K depending on the success of your product.

Can this be a source of passive income?

Well, it depends on the type of digital product and services. For example, book publishing, blogging, and Youtube can be good examples of passive income.

Does this have the potential to make you a millionaire?

Yes, definitely. In fact, this is the right path to true wealth building.

• • •

7.5 Invest in the Stock Exchange

About Stock Market Trading and Investment?

In simple terms, the stock market is a place where companies (both private and public) gather to raise money from the general public in exchange for part of their ownership.

Normally, in the stock market, investors make money in 2 ways.

- capital gains on stock prices.
- Dividends.

In short, when companies make money, investors make money, and visa-versa.

Some important terms in the stock market:

- A stock exchange or stock market is a government-regulated marketplace where stocks are bought and sold. NASDAQ, BSE, NSE, TYO, etc.
- Investors are people who invest in stocks.
- Stocks: Part of the company's ownership
- Stock trading is the process of buying and selling stocks on the stock exchange.
- Stock Brokers: authorised institutions to deal with stock market activities. If you want to start trading, then you have to go through them.
- A brokerage account is an authorised account through which you do stock trading.

Requirements to invest in the stock market?

- You need a tax identity number.
- stock trading account.
- initial capital to invest.
- knowledge of trading and investing.

Ways to Make Money in the Stock Market?

The stock market has many trading instruments for trading like

- Equity or delivery trade
- Options and future trading of derivatives
- Intraday trading
- Currency trading, etc.

Each one has a different procedure to follow to make money. For example, in delivery trading, you can make money through a capital gain or dividend.

Please read the stock market-related info for more details. Stock market rules and investment patterns vary from country to country. So I suggest you read your local stock market website for complete information.

Initial Investment or Capital

You need money for:

- Opening the trading account
- They need money for an initial capital investment.

In the beginning, you can start trading with as little as $10. But I suggest you begin with at least $100.

Time to make your first $100?

Somewhere between 4 to 9 months, based on your investment.

Yes, the stock market is a bit slow in making money.

Earning Potential

Have you ever heard of Warren Buffett, Charlie Munger, Peter Lynch, etc.? If not, then please google them.

For example, Warren Buffett is a self-made billionaire, and he made his wealth through stock market investments. The stock market has a huge potential to make money if done systematically.

Can this be a source of passive income?

Definitely yes. The stock dividend is the best form of passive income.

Does this have the potential to make you a millionaire?

Not only millionaire but it can make you a billionaire. But remember that the stock market is a long game.

• • •

7.6 Product Flipping

What is Product Flipping?

Recently, with the advent of globalisation and the online e-commerce boom, product flipping has become the new standard for making some quick bucks and some serious bucks too.

Product flipping is all about buying products for a lower price and selling them for a higher price. You can even flip websites and domains. This business has huge potential to make some quick bucks but needs smart thinking and creativity.

Some examples of product flipping

- Buying mobile phones, clothes, furniture, etc. locally at a cheap rate and re-selling them on online platforms for a higher price.
- Buying blogs or websites at a cheaper price, fixing their problems, and reselling them for profit.
- Buy products at wholesale and sell them online for a profit.

What are the prerequisites for beginning product flipping?

- laptop with an internet connection.
- some initial capital to invest.

- creative mind to identify opportunities.

Ways to Make Money from Product Flipping?

- You can directly do product flipping by purchasing at a lower price and selling at a higher one.
- You can help people do product flipping by setting an online environment for them and taking a commission per sale.
- You can make money by training people in product flipping.
- You can sell local products on any online e-commerce platform and make a commission on the sale.

Initial Investment or Capital

If you are involved directly, then you may need somewhere between 100 and 500 dollars, and again, this depends on the product you are planning to flip.

If you are working as a commission agent, then you may not need any such capital.

Time to make your first $100??

Well! It depends. But you should make your first $100 in 4 to 5 months.

Earning Potential

You can earn between $1,000 and $3,000 per month on average if you put in consistent effort.

Can this be a source of passive income?

No But, it can help you make very good active money, but not passive income.

Does this have the potential to make you a millionaire?

Yes, but it is a bit difficult. Please do not depend on this for making your first million.

• • •

7.7 Make a YouTube channel or a video blog.

About YouTube?

YouTube is a video streaming platform. It allows the public to upload legitimate videos for free for public usage and entertainment.

You can create your own free YouTube channel on YouTube and start uploading legitimate videos for public usage. If you meet YouTube's guidelines, then YouTube will allow you to monetize your channel to serve ads on it.

Requirements to start a YouTube Channel

- You need a laptop or smartphone with an internet connection.
- an email ID.
- camera to record videos.

Ways to Make Money from YouTube

- YouTube allows you to monetize your videos if you meet their guidelines. Once approved, YouTube will serve ads on your videos and pay you a portion of the advertising revenue.
- You can also do affiliate marketing.
- You can make money through paid reviews.
- You can take donations.
- You can sell merchandise.
- You can licence your video content.
- Money, as well as name and fame, can be obtained through YouTube.

Initial Investment/Capital

If you have a laptop or mobile with a camera and an internet connection, then you do not need any capital.

If you are serious about YouTube, then I suggest you invest in video editing software and some good quality cameras.

Time to make your first $100?

It depends on what source of income you are dependent on and how popular your channel is.

Earning Potential

Some of the most famous YouTube channels make money in the millions.

With consistency and popularity, you can make around 2000 to 5000 dollars per month. Again, it all depends on what your source of income is.

Can this be a source of passive income?

Yes, but you may have to keep on uploading videos.

Does this have the potential to make you a millionaire?

Yes. But very few make it.

Some famous YouTube channels that make a good amount of money are:

- Jake Paul
- PewDiePie, etc

• • •

7.8 Online Education

About Online Education:

Online education is not only booming but has also become a necessity. Online education is where you can learn or teach through online means remotely.

Ways to teach online:

- You can create the courses and let people join and learn them.
- Live Classes

Live teaching platforms:

- Skype App
- Zoom App

- Google Video Chat, etc.

Platform to build courses and sell them

- Udemy
- teachable
- LinkedIn Learning, etc.
- YouTube
- Share videos through Google Drive, etc.

The best part of online education is that it has brought down the cost of education.

For example, learning photography classes offline used to cost more than $1,000, but now you can attend and learn in-depth photography courses for as little as $200, and on some platforms, as little as $10.

Online education advantages:

- global audience.
- recorded teaching material for offline reference.
- No need for a classroom investment.
- You have the opportunity to update the course material when required.
- It helps students discuss the topic even after many days through comment sections, etc.

What are the prerequisites for beginning online education?

- You need a laptop with an internet connection.
- camera and a good-quality voice recorder.
- Mastery of the subject matter in which you teach
- video editing software.

Ways to Make Money from Online Education?

- You can create courses and upload them to online teaching platforms like Udemy, Teachable, YouTube, etc.
- You can take online live classes.
- You can take mock interviews.
- Help students prepare for exams.

Initial Investment or Capital

The cost of the camera, audio recording device, and video editing software will be your required capital.

Time to make your first $100?

You can make the first $100 somewhere between 2 and 5 months.

Earning Potential

Established online tutors make an average of $2000 to $5,000 per month.

Can this be a source of passive income?

Yes, this is one of the many passive income sources.

Does this have the potential to make you a millionaire?

Yes. Many successful online tutors make money in the millions.

• • •

7.9 Freelancing

What is freelancing?

Freelancing is a kind of self-employment. Here, people work for themselves and are not employed by any company or organization. Freelancers work on projects in which they are interested and have expertise.

In freelancing, you find your own job. You bid for the projects you are interested in, complete the project, and get the payment. This kind of model really suits many individuals who would like to work once in a while.

Some of the best freelancing websites to find on-demand jobs are:

- Fiverr.com
- Upwork.com
- PeoplePerHour.com
- Freelancer.com, etc

Prerequisites for Beginning Freelancing

A laptop with an internet connection and knowledge of any specific technology to work with. That is it.

Some ideas that are most suitable for freelancing:

- Image and video editing
- Content creation.
- SEO.
- Audiobook
- Book editing
- Development of software applications
- Development of mobile applications
- Cover designer.
- Audiobook, etc.

Ways to Make Money from Freelancing?

You have to get the work from the mentioned sources and complete the task to get paid. That is it.

Initial Investment/Capital

If you have a laptop and an internet connection, then that is more than enough.

Time to make your first $100?

It completely depends on you.

Earning Potential

Good. With only 20 hours of work per week, you can easily earn $500 to $800 per month.

Can this be a source of passive income?

No This is an active income source.

Does this have the potential to make you a millionaire?

I genuinely doubt it.

• • •

7.10 Drop-Shipping

What is Drop-Shipping?

Though drop-shipping looks like product flipping, it has a slight difference.

This is a retail fulfilment method where the seller does not keep the store to maintain the stock he is selling; rather, he purchases the item once the order is confirmed and fulfils it to the destination directly.

In simple words, being the middle man between the real buyer and seller, or some kind of fake seller,

Some drop-shipping websites

- Shopify.
- Amazon
- Alibaba.

What are the prerequisites for starting drop-shipping?

- laptop with the internet.
- Suitable training.

Ways to Make Money from Drop-Shipping

You will list the product on an e-commerce website at a higher price than the product that is being sold on another e-commerce platform at a lower price. Through the entire process, buyers will not realise that there is a middle man in between.

Well! I tried my best to explain this in simple words. But still, if you find it difficult to understand, then I suggest you watch some YouTube videos on this subject.

Note: In some countries or cities, drop shipping may be illegal, so please check before starting this business.

Initial Investment/Capital

Whatever it costs for you to arrange a laptop with an internet connection.

Time to make your first $100?

You should make your first $100 within 5 months based on sales.

Earning Potential

Successful drop-shippers make an average of $5k to $20k per month.

Can this be a source of passive income?

Not completely. You need continuous monitoring for the success of this business.

Does this have the potential to make you a millionaire?

Yes, many successful drop-shippers made millions.

• • •

7.11 Podcasting

What is podcasting?

Distribution of audio files through the internet, either in live form or in recorded form, is called podcasting.

In podcasting, a person will be voice-casting the selected subjects, like motivation, success factors, stories, interviews, etc.

Some of the best podcast hosting websites and apps are:

- Audioboom.
- Fusebox.
- Simplecast.
- SoundCloud
- PodBean, etc.

What Are the Prerequisites for Starting a Podcast?

- Be a master of the subject you want to talk about.
- Voice Recorder

- free voice editing software like Audacity.
- You can even use a laptop or mobile phone for recording, editing, uploading, or hosting the podcast.

Ways to Make Money from Podcasting?

- You can make money through ads that can be played in between the podcasts.
- Paid podcasts
- Audiobooks.
- Make money on your podcast downloads, etc

Initial Investment/Capital

Nil. You can start your podcasting on your mobile phone with an internet connection.

Time to make your first $100?

Making money in podcasting is a bit of a slow process. Usually, it may take 5 to 12 months before you make your first $100.

Earning Potential

Though a successful podcaster makes money in the millions, the average successful podcaster can make anywhere from $500 to $2000 per month.

Can this be a source of passive income?

Yes. This can generate passive income. However, earning potential is low.

Does this have the potential to make you a millionaire?

Yes. But very few manage to make money in the millions.

• • •

7.12 Book Publishing

About Book Publishing:

Book publishing (which is self-explanatory) has been around with us for many years. But what has changed is the way the book is being published, read, and sold.

Now you can write, read, and sell books in digital form. (In the form of soft copy like Pdf, Word Docs, Epub, etc. format).

With the advent of the internet and digital platforms, book publishing has moved from physical publishing to digital publishing form, and this is what gives us an immense opportunity to make money.

But, how?

Books can now be published in digital form. Since it is in digital form, you can publish books on the internet, and within minutes it is available to everyone globally. With this, you can reduce your printing costs and reach worldwide readers within a couple of minutes.

Also, you can publish books in physical form through on-demand publishing platforms like Amazon Kindle Publications, Kobo, Draft2Digital, etc.

Book Publishing Prerequisites

- laptop with an internet connection.
- book publishing tools.
- interest in writing books (you can also hire writers).
- Knowledge of book publishing (I suggest you take some good courses online or read books related to this subject before publishing your first book).
- good vocabulary in the English language or in any native language in which you want to publish a book. But since English is a language spoken and understood worldwide, I suggest you write books in the English language.

Ways to Make Money from Book Publishing?

- You can make money through different means.
- You can self-publish books through on-demand publishing platforms like Amazon KDP, Draft2Digital, etc. (By the way, these platforms take a cut from your sales. It is just like profit sharing.
- You can help others to publish their books and make a commission out of it.
- You can teach book publishing and make money as a tutor.
- There are many more ways, like affiliate marketing, placing ads on your books, etc. Again, it all depends on your creativity in making money.

Please read the third party of the publisher's manual for more information on what is allowed and what is not.

Initial Investment or Capital

You do not need any investment except for a laptop and the internet.

All you need is good vocabulary and creative writing skills.

Time to make your first $100??

Depends. But, with 2 to 3 high-content books with appreciable content, you should be making your first $100 in 2 to 3 months.

Earning Potential

With 10 to 15 high-quality books online, you can easily make $2000 to $3000 per month.

Can this be a source of passive income?

Yes, this is perhaps one of the best sources of passive income.

Does this have the potential to make you a millionaire?

Yes, the world's bestselling authors do make money in the millions.

(If you are interested in learning about book publishing, then check out my book on Book Publishing and Related Topics.)

• • •

7.13 WFH Jobs, Part-Time or Full-Time

About Regular and Part-time WFH Jobs?

Many companies permit their employees to work from home full time. Although not all domains suit this job type. But there are many which are especially suited for WFH (Work from Home) type jobs.

Domains which are suited for WFH type jobs include:

- software development.
- Software Testing
- digital marketing.
- Online trainers
- software support jobs.
- Teleservices jobs
- Finance and Accounting (backend).
- Data entry.
- data analysis.
- Data visualisation
- etc

Some domains are not suited for WFH type jobs:

- Lab support jobs
- Mechanical jobs
- jobs in automobiles.
- jobs in sales and marketing.
- In general, jobs that demand physical presence or travel are

Keeping these things in mind, whenever you join any organization, make sure you negotiate the WFH facility before joining full-time or signing any contract for part-time jobs.

What are the prerequisites for starting WFH software jobs?

- You should be in a domain that suits this type of job culture.

- You should be competitive enough to perform WFH jobs.
- You should bargain for WFH (Please keep in mind that not everyone is given the opportunity to WFH, and in many industries, companies will not encourage employees to WFH for a variety of reasons).
- You should have a sound internet connection with a power backup facility.

Ways to Make Money from WFH Software Jobs

- Well, the main source of income is through salary.
- You can also work as a part-time consultant and negotiate a fixed amount for that.

Initial Investment/Capital

Whatever it costs for a laptop and internet connection.

Time to make your first $100?

It will not apply here since you will be getting a fixed amount as a salary.

Earning Potential

Whatever salary you negotiate with your company,

Can this be a source of passive income?

No, you have to keep working to make money.

Does this have the potential to make you a millionaire?

It all depends on you. But in normal cases, no.

• • •

7.14 Photographie, videography, and audio files

About Photography Business?

In the olden days, we used to use a camera with film to take pictures. Since the camera roll and films were costly, the scope for an experiment in photography was very small. Also, the camera was costly and was available to very few people.

Those days are gone.

With the technological boom, the photography and videography industries too have changed a lot.

Here are the four things that changed these industries:

- With a digital camera and memory cards, with which you can now take as many pics as possible and even experiment with photography techniques. Also, a memory card is reusable, so the cost of photography has come down drastically.
- Mass manufacturing and automation have brought down the cost of the camera as well as the memory card. At present, you can buy a good quality camera with a memory card at a price as low as $1000.
- With the smartphone boom, you can take pictures as well as record audio and video on your smartphone with considerable quality.

- With the Internet, online markets, and digital banking, you can now buy and sell photos, videos, and audio clips with a single mouse click from any part of the world. This technology has opened up a huge global market for photographers.

What are the prerequisites for starting a photography business?

- You have to learn photography and videography skills.
- You should learn photo and video editing skills.
- Travel around your home or some local tourist attractions to get some good pics.
- Learn how to sell online.

Ways to Make Money from the Photography Business?

- On-line photo sales
- Sell videos.
- You can sell nature sounds, animal sounds, rain sounds, water sounds, etc.
- Teach photography and videography online on a platform like Teachable, Udemy, YouTube, etc.
- Offer photography eBooks for sale.
- You can also make money from editing photos and videos for others.
- Affiliate Marketing
- Work for the Media

Initial Investment/Capital

This requires a little bit of investment.

- You have to invest in some good, professional cameras.
- Invest in photo editing and video editing software.
- You may have to invest in some camera accessories like a stand, memory card, etc.

Time to make your first $100?

It usually takes between 5 to 8 months, based on your efforts.

Earning Potential

between 500 and 4,000 dollars per month.

Can this be a source of passive income?

Yes. You can make money by selling photos and videos online on sites like Shutterstock, etc.

Does this have the potential to make you a millionaire?

Yes, but normally it is difficult.

• • •

7.15 E-commerce (selling products online)

About E-Commerce Business?

Before the internet era, selling products was mostly limited to local areas. Whatever you have to sell has to be sold at the local market or to traders. Also, the choice of products was limited because of a lack of global market exposure.

But now, time has changed a lot. We have global delivery networks like Amazon, Alibaba, etc. We have an online payment facility; we have internet and smartphone facilities at hand. With this, the e-commerce industry has boomed like no other business in the last 100 years.

Now you can start an e-commerce business through e-commerce stores like Amazon, Alibaba, etc., which have a global market and sell your products online.

Some of the items which you can sell online include:

- You can sell your own homemade products.
- You can sell products like packed food items, groceries, medicine (with a proper license), mechanical tools , etc. Normally, whatever you can buy from a market outside can be found on an e-commerce platform.
- What you cannot sell are restricted medicines, drugs, and illegal products as marked by the government and other items which are banned by your government.

What are the prerequisites for starting an e-commerce business?

- You need a laptop and an internet connection.
- You need in-depth knowledge of the e-commerce business.
- You may have to register a company if your local law says so.

- You need to do some market research and finalise the items to sell online.
- You also need some initial capital to buy or create products.

Ways to Make Money from E-commerce business?

- You can sell your own product (physical product or digital product).
- You can import and sell products locally.
- You can sell local market items and take a commission.
- You can help others set up their e-commerce business.
- You can be an e-commerce tutor.
- You can sell a book on e-commerce.

Initial Investment/Capital

It depends on what you want to sell, and usually, you may need capital of between 300 and 5000 dollars.

Also, you may have to spend money on registering your brand if it is demanded by your local regulations.

Time to make your first $100?

Usually between 3 to 5 months.

Earning Potential

The earning potential of e-commerce businesses is huge and growing even faster every day.

With good products, you can easily make between 2000 and 10,000 dollars per month or even more.

Can this be a source of passive income?

This is a quasi-passive income business. because you have to keep working on it for refilling stocks, advertisements, handling service or return calls, etc.

But, if you streamline and automate it, you can convert it into a passive business.

Does this have the potential to make you a millionaire?

Yes, yes, and yes.

• • •

I have covered the above-mentioned options in detail because they are very important and have a huge potential to make a good amount of money. They are, however, a drop in the ocean.There are many more ways through which you can make money from home through online means.

Here are some more ways of making money from home:

- E-Assistance: Remote Digital Assistance.
- Domain Flipping: Buying and selling domains
- You can exploit security flaws in well-known websites and software to bring them to their attention and earn a good living.
- Online surveys: complete the surveys and get paid.
- Data Entry
- Photoshop and Digital Art.
- Manager, Social Media.
- Social Media Marketing.
- SEO Expert
- E-Friend.

- Online priest
- Be an assistant to the digital illiterate.

Well, this list will go on and on. For the above, you can do more research and explore it.

Making money online is the new standard now. Now the world is moving from offline standards to online standards.

If you are not digital literate, then sooner or later you will lose this trend and be left behind by new online junkies.

But wait, though the internet and digital are the future, But that is not the only future. There are many offline ways through which you can still make money. We will see those in detail in the next section.

CHAPTER VIII

Making Money through Offline means

Though online methods are best suited for making money while sitting at home, that does not mean you cannot make money offline. There are hundreds of ways through which you can make money while sitting (logically) at home.

For example, below is a list that covers some of the important ways to make money from home.

- Tailoring.
- Cloud kitchen
- Home-schooling and tuition classes
- Stock Market: You can trade through phone calls or mobile applications.
- Courier collector: collect the courier on behalf of someone else and charge for that.
- Food Parcel Service (Lunch or Dinner): You can run a mini canteen at your home by cooking limited food items and serving them as a parcel like cloud kitchen.
- Prepare snacks and food eateries: You can prepare food eateries and snacks for bakeries or food stores in wholesale quantities. You can also prepare for functions like birthdays, anniversaries, small parties, etc.
- Because of a lack of reading interest among people, many public libraries are vanishing. You can use this opportunity to run a mini library with a reading facility. You can charge a fixed amount for it.
- Yoga, fitness, dance, aerobics, Zumba, etc. classes
- Flip old vehicles and furniture.
- Grocery shop

- home-run bakery.
- Homemade crafts and clothes
- Manage a Small Neighborly Coffee Shop
- Run kindergarten.
- Rent jewelry: Nowadays, people are going crazy over 1-gram gold jewelry. But they are not interested in keeping them for a long time. You can buy some jewellery (which is low-cost and affordable) and rent it for a fixed price. This is an emerging and booming business among women's self-help groups.
- beauty parlours, spas, and salons.
- Many people who do not have time or facilities to cook at home prefer home food if available. You can have a contract with a select few to feed them daily for a fixed price. This is a win-win model. This model is famous in metro cities around the world.
- Mobile and electronics repair and services.
- You can do candid photography for your selected customers and business clients. Many local families prefer a photographer who is trustworthy and neighbor-friendly. You must use this to your advantage if you love photography.
- cooking class.
- Flipping of artwork and painting
- Being a real estate broker has the potential to earn millions of dollars.
- Be an interior designer.
- Laundry services
- Rent costumes: Many people, especially in theatre and related work, need lots of costumes on a rental basis. This is also a very good business model in metro cities.
- Sell costumes among local communities: You can understand the local community's taste and buy the clothes at wholesale and sell them for a profit.
- Network marketing has the potential to earn millions of dollars. Make sure you understand this business model before entering it.
- If you are a doctor, you can run a home clinic.

- wedding planner
- The Travel Planner
- Home Stay Service
- home gardening trainer.
- Be Florist
- Rental Business (Real Estate)
- On a daily basis, many people require a printer and other internet services.You can provide that service at your home. This is best suited for locations like remote villages or small towns.
- antique shop.
- Home run medical therapy.
- Run a small garage for bike and car repair.
- Rent a bicycle, etc.

I will not be covering each one of the above in detail because that makes no sense as these are self-explanatory.

But what you have to understand here is, offline means of making money from home have some serious limitations as well as serious advantages too.

Offline mode has the following advantages:

- Online learning requires big learning curves and a logical-thinking mindset, and this is what makes people give up early in their career. But offline does not involve much of a learning curve. If you are the one who thinks online is a bit messy to learn, then I suggest you first get started in offline mode and make some bucks, and then take up classes to learn about online business and then jump in.
- It's a bit easier to make money in offline mode as compared to online.
- Offline mode is socially friendly and you get the chance to mingle with real people.

- Offline mode keeps your life simple. Trust me, online mode sometimes gets really messy and irritating when it comes to technicality and configuration issues.
- Offline mode helps you build and maintain a routine habit, which is very difficult in online mode. For example, if you run a local bakery, you can maintain a fixed time. But if you start blogging, then you end up working without any schedule or timing.
- You do not have to deal with online payment-related issues.
- Getting recognition is a bit simpler in offline mode than in online mode.

You can count on many advantages like this. But, it has some serious disadvantages too.

Offline Means Have the Following Drawbacks:

Like advantages, being offline also has serious disadvantages. Some of the important disadvantages are listed below.

- Customer Reach: Per my analysis, perhaps this is the biggest disadvantage. The moment you get offline, all you are left with is your friends and neighbours and some rare visitors who may be interested in your product or services.
- With online, you can reach almost the entire globe where internet facilities are available, but with offline, your products and services become accessible only in the local vicinity. This drastically reduces your chances of making money.
- Earning Capacity: Earning capacity is frequently reduced and limited as a result of poor customer reach.
- You may have to run local advertisements to make your business visible to your friends and to your surroundings.
- You have fewer chances to promote and grow your business.
- Often, offline businesses are not passive. Like online businesses like blogging or e-books where you do it once and leave it to

grow on its own, here you have to be with the business each and every day to make it run.

- An offline business is best suited for those who value consistency and prefer to be present in front of their business at all times.
- Offline business needs patience.
- Growth is limited.

CHAPTER IX

Making Money Through Hybrid Means

For many, it is a bit confusing about whether to start an online or offline mode of business. Let me make this task easy for you.

There is always a middle path in everything you do in life. So does making money from home.

The offline mode of business is limited in reach as well as in earning potential, but gives you peace of mind from some serious online business technical challenges.

At the same time, though the online business model is a bit challenging for people who are technically not so sound (do not feel sorry for this; there is nothing wrong with not knowing these things), it is good for passive income generation and helps you make a very good amount of money for a long time.

Here is what you can do.

- If you are not comfortable with an online business or if you have any technical limitations, then first you start an offline business or job from home and make money.
- Save a little money from that business and invest it in acquiring digital knowledge like understanding and using computers, using the internet, learning MS Word, PDF, Excel, etc., using social media, Google, etc.
- Now from there, you extend that business to the online world.
- If you are still not comfortable, then you can pay someone else to take your business online and maintain it.
- This is the most stable and consistent way to make money from home.

CHAPTER X

Summary

In short, making money from home is definitely possible and, in fact, this is the growing trend now. But before jumping in, you may have to analyse your strengths and weaknesses first.

I suggest you first understand your technical skills, your strength, and your interests. If you are technically sound, then go ahead and start working online. But if you are not at all interested in online, then offline ways are enough to survive too.

But, if you have a long-term view on making money from home, then I suggest you move online sooner or later because this is the new future.

CHAPTER XI

Disclaimer

All the methods and ideas mentioned above are purely my personal work and derived from my personal experiences and research. Though they are a good way to make money from home, nothing is guaranteed in that aspect since making money from home depends on so many other factors too.

Please consider this book as a reference and grow your knowledge of the selected topic even further before making any serious investment of time or money or both.

Although the author and publisher of this book have made every effort to ensure that the information in this book is correct at present, the author and publisher do not assume and hereby disclaim any liability to any party for any loss, damage, or disruption caused by errors or omissions, whether such errors or omissions result from negligence, accident, or any other cause.

Printed by Libri Plureos GmbH in Hamburg,
Germany